BABA TREASURE CHEST

A Collection of Modern Bulgarian Tales

by

Ronesa Aveela

Illustrated by Nelinda

BENDIDEIA
PUBLISHING

Dedication

This book is dedicated to all those who have ever believed that dreams and fairy tales can come true.

Ronesa Aveela

THE Miracle Stork

Illustrated by Nelinda

A "Baba Treasure Chest" story

Rada pumped her feet, rising higher than she'd ever dared swing before. The wind lifted her wild black curls, spreading them out like a cape. She yearned to touch the clouds that ambled across the sky. In her mind, they transformed into the animals she was going to see at the zoo.

"Rada," her mother said from the doorway. "Grandma Neda called. Her bus will be here any moment."

"Yeah!" Rada held her legs out straight to slow the swing, leaning back as she watched fluffy white animals parade across the sky. Rhino. Tiger. Stork. Monkey. She lay on the swing until a bus squeaked to a stop and steps echoed on the driveway.

"Baba!" She leaped toward the white-haired woman bundled up against the chilly spring air.

An orange-spotted cat beat her to Baba's side. The feline rubbed against the woman's legs, purring all the while, as she marked another human as her own.

"Murka," Rada said, out of breath. "I wanted to welcome Baba first."

The girl wrapped her arms around her grandmother and squeezed tight.

Grandma Neda held Rada at arm's length. "My big beautiful girl. Look at how you've grown. You'll be taller than me soon."

"Baba, did you know they have a huge white tiger at the zoo? And a baby monkey. I can't wait to see them."

"Lunch first, Rada. Welcome, Grandma Neda." Her mother disappeared into the house.

The elderly woman sighed and whispered, "I'm glad you still call me by the old Bulgarian name. Your parents seem to have forgotten all our ways since they've lived in America."

"They let me make this." Rada smiled big and held out her hand, where an amulet of red and white twisted threads dangled around her wrist. Tiny white bird beads attached to the tassels swung like they were flying.

"But did they tell you stories about your martenitsa?"

"No." Rada frowned. "I like stories. Will you tell me some?"

"Yes, later. Let's go inside now," Baba said as she took Rada's hand, "and I'll remind your parents of our customs."

Wind burst into the house with them, scattering papers off a small table in the hallway.

"Brr. Quickly, close the door," Rada's mother said. "The groundhog predicted six more weeks of winter, but it's already been almost eight."

"Hmph. Groundhog." Baba waved her finger under her daughter-in-law's nose. "Where's your red? You've made Baba Marta angry by not wearing any."

"Who's Baba Marta?" Rada looked from her grandmother to her mother. "And why do we have to wear red?"

Baba crossed her arms over her chest. "See? Do you want your child growing up ignorant of her heritage?"

"We've had this conversation before. We don't want her ridiculed." Rada's mother turned toward her daughter. "Lunch is ready."

Rada swung her legs, kicking the wooden rungs at the bottom of her chair. "Baba, who's Baba Marta? Why does she get mad if you don't wear red?"

"Her name means 'Grandmother March,' and she's an old woman like me who wants things to go her way." Baba snuck a glance at her son who walked in.

"Welcome, Mom. So glad you can visit for a while." He bent to kiss her cheek. "Sorry to interrupt."

"I was starting to tell Rada about how Baba Marta controls the weather for this month."

"Mother ... don't." Rada's father whispered harshly, giving her a cold stare.

Baba turned her own icy eyes toward her son. "It's time to teach her so she knows about our customs. She doesn't have to give up one way of life in order to live another. She can have both old and new traditions."

"I won't listen to your fairy tales." He pushed his chair back and stomped out of the room.

Tears swelled in Rada's eyes. "Why's Daddy mad? Baba only wanted to tell me a story."

Rada's mother lightly stroked her daughter's forearm. "When Daddy came to live in America as a boy, he had a hard time. Kids teased him for his broken speech and called him ignorant and stupid for his beliefs."

Baba snorted. "The only ignorant ones are those who refuse to accept others who are different."

"Maybe you're right ... Baba. I'll talk with him. It's time to embrace who we are." Rada's mother squeezed Baba's hand, kissed her daughter on the top of her head, and left.

Baba lifted Rada's head and wiped away the tears. "Do you want me to tell you now?"

Rada sniffed. "If it's okay."

"Yes, it'll be okay. Your father needs a kick in the pants to make him think."

Rada giggled. "He might not like that."

"No, he might not." Baba cleared her throat. "Baba Marta is old, even older than me. Poor thing is hunchbacked and limps along, leaning on a stick. But she *is* as grumpy as I am, and demands people pay attention to her."

"You're not grumpy, but Daddy does say you're stubborn."

"I am that." Baba nodded. "But this other Baba made *everyone* do as she wanted. If people displeased her in any way, she'd send blizzards during March."

"Do you think it's so cold today because Mommy didn't wear red and made Baba Marta mad?"

"Most likely. Red's Marta's favorite color. It's like the warm sun shining down on us. The more red we show her, the nicer she makes the weather."

Rada wiggled in her seat. "Then I'm going to wear my red jacket, red scarf, *and* red mittens when we go. I think it's too warm, but Mommy gets all fussy that I might get cold."

"You'll also want to make sure your room is clean before we leave."

"Why?"

"Baba Marta likes everything to be neat. Her own house is immaculate."

Rada covered her mouth to suppress a laugh. She looked at the door and whispered, "Maybe that's the story Daddy didn't like. Mommy says he's messy."

"He was as a child, too," Baba said. "Marta wasn't angry all the time, though. We have a saying that when she smiles, the sun shines and spring flowers blossom. Now finish your lunch. I'll tell you about martenitsi when we're on the bus."

On the warm bus, Rada unbuttoned her jacket and took off her gloves. She bounced on the seat and stuck her nose on the cool window. "Baba, look at that cute puppy. Mommy promised to get me one next year when I'm eight. I'm sure Murka won't mind. And look at—"

Baba smiled. "Do you want to hear more about why we wear martenitsi?"

"Oh, yes, please." Rada sat still, her hands clasped in her lap, with her feet swinging under the seat.

"Besides being fun to make—" Baba started.

"It was sooo much fun. Mommy and me made them a few weeks ago, but she said I couldn't wear mine until the next day." Rada pouted.

"That's because you're supposed to make it the night before Baba Marta Den, which is March first, but not wear it until the next day," Baba said. "It's a special day devoted to the grumpy old woman. She'd be angry if you wore it earlier."

"Why didn't we make it on her day, then?"

Baba sighed. "Years ago in Bulgaria, when people still believed in our traditions, everyone made martenitsi the night before Baba Marta Den and left them tied to a rosebush. That way, when the sun rose, its rays would fill the amulets with magical powers."

Rada leaned closer, her eyes wide. "Magic? What can they do?"

"They keep away evil spirits and disasters," Baba said with sincerity.

Rada looked around, then whispered. "I don't see any ghosts so it must work."

"Today's the day we take them off—"

Rada reached for her grandmother's hand. "But won't bad things be able to get us?"

"No," Baba said, squeezing Rada's hand. "The martenitsi will protect you all year if you tie them to a tree today."

"Why today?"

"It's Blagovets," Baba said, "a day we officially celebrate the arrival of spring, which is a magical time. Flowers and trees blossom with life. Your Diado often said no one could work on this day—not even animals, birds, or insects."

"Really?"

"Yes, it's a day filled with enchantment and mystery, like Christmas. Instead of celebrating the birth of our Lord, all creatures celebrate Nature giving birth to spring."

"So do we get presents?"

Baba laughed. "Not for this holiday. The gift you get is protection. Since we haven't seen any of the other signs of spring yet—"

"What signs?" Rada bounced in her seat again.

"A stork or cuckoo. Flowering trees. Those are the main ones."

"We'll see a stork at the zoo, won't we?"

"Yes, dear." Baba looked out the window, and her voice broke. "Every March twenty-fifth, your Diado and I came here to tie our amulets on a tree in front of the stork's aviary. We sat on a bench by a flowerbed filled with yellow-and-red-striped tulips. The charms looked so lovely as they danced in the wind like butterflies."

"I don't remember him," Rada said. "Do you miss Grandpa?"

"I do." She wiped away tears. "But I have your mother, and your father, who reminds me of Diado so much. And I have you. You share his radiant smile and sparkling eyes."

Rada smiled bigger. "Like this?"

"Exactly." Baba patted Rada's hand. "Did you know if you tie your amulet to a fruit tree, the magic goes into the tree, and it'll produce a lot of fruit?"

"I love apples." Rada licked her lips. "Magical apples would be even better."

"If you make a wish when you tie your amulet to the tree, it'll come true."

"It will? I have to think what to wish for." Rada twirled the tassels on her martenitsa.

"Some people do other things with martenitsi."

"Like what?"

"Throwing them in a river so all their troubles will float away."

"I have to tell Mommy. She worries a lot about me and Daddy."

"When I was a girl, we used to make predictions with our martenitsi." Baba closed her eyes for a moment. "On March twenty-fifth, we placed them under a stone. Nine days later, we went back to see what kind of insects covered the charms."

"Insects, yuck." Rada stuck out her tongue.

"They're a necessary part of life," Baba said.

"Why did you care if insects were on them?"

"Each type indicated a different future. Beetles, ants, worms, and ladybugs meant health and success. Ladybugs were my favorite."

"I love ladybugs, too, especially the quilt you made me that shows bunches of them."

"Sometimes there were bad signs, like snakes and spiders."

Rada shuddered. "I don't think I'll try that. I wouldn't want to find those creepy things."

Baba let out a deep breath. "No, I don't recommend it. That's one of the things that turned your father away from our traditions. Some boys came with him when he lifted the stone. One mean boy threw a rubber spider into the hole and told your father he deserved to be sick and have problems all year if he believed such nonsense."

"Oh, poor Daddy."

"Yes, my poor baby," Baba said with sadness. "Ah, we're at our stop."

fter looking at pictures of new arrivals at the zoo posted on a large board, Rada and her grandmother stopped at a shop to buy food to feed the animals. Holding the bag against her chest, Rada skipped over to the monkeys.

"Wait for me, dear. I can't keep up with you." Baba caught her breath and made her way along the stone path.

Rada plunked a peanut into a metal bowl at the base of a pole. A monkey darted out of his little hut and pulled the rope up. He shelled the nut and crunched on it, then lowered the bowl. Looking over the edge of his platform, the monkey screeched.

"Does that mean he wants more?" Rada asked.

Baba covered her ears. "I'm sure he does. Put a few more in if you want. Otherwise, he'll keep screaming. I'll give him a treat, too."

She reached into her pocket, pulled out something wrapped in paper, and dropped it into the bowl along with the peanuts.

Rada pointed her phone at the monkey and took pictures of him eating peanuts. He popped Baba's treat into his mouth, then spat it out, screeching at them. Getting nothing more, he left to climb through a rope jungle, performing acrobatics.

"What did you give him, Baba?"

Her grandmother showed her.

"A cough drop?" Rada giggled. "No wonder he didn't like it."

"Monkeys must get sick sometimes, too." She put the cough drop back into her pocket. "He'll eat it when he gets a sore throat."

Rada glanced back at the monkey. "I think he's mad at us now, so let's go see more animals."

They stopped at the parrot house, then visited the cheetahs and other wild cats.

"Let's sit for a while," Baba said, a little out of breath. "I'll tell you a tale about martenitsi before we go see the storks."

"Yes, please!" Rada scrambled onto the bench.

"This is the story of Penda and Pijo. They're the little yarn dolls that some people attach to their martenitsi."

"Those were too hard for me, so I used these stork beads." Rada swung the charm, making the birds dangle.

"Those are still lovely," Baba said. "Maybe when you know more about Penda and Pijo, your mother will help you make them."

"Who are they?"

"Pijo was a ruler in a faraway land, and Penda was the woman he loved. One day a bad man captured Penda. Pijo didn't know what to do. He had to rule his kingdom, so he couldn't leave. He sent out carrier pigeons looking for her, hoping someone would answer his pleas, but the birds didn't return."

"He'll have to try something else," Rada said. "Daddy tells me to never give up."

"That's right. Pijo sent his most-trusted soldier to look for her," Baba continued. "The journey was long and took many months. No one the soldier met had seen Penda. In the spring, he saw an old woman and eleven old men sitting by a well."

Rada shook her head. "That's a funny place to sit."

"They were tired from trying to pull a bucket of water from the well, so the soldier helped them. The old woman told him she was Baba Marta, and the men were her brothers, the other months of the year."

"Cool," Rada said. "It would be nice to have a brother."

"I'm sure." Baba smiled. "Marta told the soldier he'd find what he was looking for because he had been kind to them. Soon after that, he came across the house where Penda was held prisoner."

"Yeah! He's going to rescue her."

"He did. He fought with the bad man and defeated him. When he released Penda, she found one of the pigeons Pijo had sent. She tied a message to its leg with a white thread, saying she was safe and was returning to him. But the bird hurt its wing on a tree branch when it stopped to rest. Blood dripped onto the thread, turning it red in places."

"Yuck." Rada scrunched her nose.

"Pijo didn't care. When the bird returned to him with the message, he took the blood-stained thread from the pigeon's foot and attached it to his shirt. He wore it until Penda returned home, as a reminder that she was safe. And that's why we make martenitsi with red and white thread."

"I love that story. Thank you for telling me, Baba." Rada rose to her knees on the bench and hugged her grandmother.

"I'm looking forward to seeing that old tree," Baba said as she and Rada made their way down the path to the bird aviary after visiting various exotic animals. "Every year since your Diado and I started putting our martenitsi on it, more and more people have done the same. I think people make a special trip just to view the tree with its dancing amulets. They've made a new tradition from our old one."

"I'm glad I get to see it with you." Rada twirled around.

Baba took a deep breath of the cool air. "Spring is such a lovely time of year."

"I love it, too. The flowers bloom, the sun rises early, we have school vacation, and Mommy and Daddy take me to fun places."

"Did you know today is the day Samodivi travel back from Dragon Village to return to our world?"

Rada tilted her head to the side. "Samodivi? Dragon Village?"

"Yes, I suppose your parents never told you about them, either." Baba walked with hunched shoulders. "Dragon Village is a place where not only dragons live during the winter, but also Samodivi and Rusalki, whom you'd probably call mermaids."

"Like Ariel?"

"Yes, her and others."

"Have you ever been there?" Rada stopped dancing. "Maybe Mommy and Daddy will bring me there on our vacation."

Baba chuckled. "I haven't. I'm afraid only the magpie knows how to find the doorway to that magical land. If I could, I'd like to see the Samodivi."

"Why? Do they have fish tails like the Ru— mermaids?"

"Rusalki. No. Samodivi are beautiful nymphs who live mostly in forests. They love to dance and sing at night. Their silk robes are as delicate as a spider's web and as dazzling as a moonbeam."

Rada bit her lower lip. "What's a nymph?"

"It's a type of fairy."

"Are they tiny and have wings like the Blue Fairy in Pinocchio?"

"No, they look like us except they have pale skin, so sometimes it's hard to tell they're magical creatures," Baba said. "Their hair is curly and long. Most people say their hair is blonde, but I've seen pictures of them with auburn and black hair as well."

Rada swished her dark curls. "So I could be a Samodiva someday?"

Baba laughed. "I'd rather you stay a little girl for a while longer. Samodivi might be beautiful, but they like to play tricks on people, too."

"I don't like being mean to others."

"They're not always bad. They protect plants and animals," Baba said. "I have a book you can read to learn more about them when you're older. It's called *Mystical Emona*, a beautiful love story between a Samodiva and an artist."

"I want to see a nymph, too."

"If you hear a cuckoo sing, you'll know one is nearby."

"Maybe we'll see a cuckoo, and it'll sing to us. I'm sure Samodivi come to the zoo if they like animals." Rada grabbed her grandmother's hand. "Let's hurry so we can see."

As they got closer, Rada let her grandmother's hand slip and ran toward a display of yellow-and-red tulips, surrounded by pearly-white snow-drops. "Baba, I think the storks are here."

She read a sign by the glassed-in enclosure. "Eu-ro-pe-an Stork. I was right! And look, inside is a bird with a long pointed beak that looks like a carrot. Why do they call it Eu-ro-pe-an?"

Baba looked around. Dark shadows and sadness replaced her smile. She answered half-heartedly, "They come from my homeland. You'll only find them in the zoo because they don't live here." Baba continued to turn her head. "But this can't be the right place."

"It is. See the flowers and bench you and Diado sat on. And the stork. I see its nest. I wonder if it has baby birdies in it."

"It's not right. The tree ... our tree is gone! It was here last year." She shuffled toward the bench. Tears leaked around her lids when she closed her eyes.

"Baba, what's wrong?" Rada sat on the bench and put her hands over her grandmother's. "Maybe the tree was sick, and someone took it away. I saw a man do that once to a tree on our street. It kept dropping big branches in the road. There are other pretty things here besides the tree."

"It was special." Baba choked on her words. "It was a memory of Diado, and now that's gone, too."

Rada snuggled next to Baba, still holding her hands. She let the birds entertain her while her grandmother leaned back with her eyes closed.

"Baba?" Rada said softly, "Did you do other fun things on Baba Marta Den when you were little?"

"Yes, we had lots of rituals."

"What kind?" Rada wiggled on the bench.

"Bieme tigani."

"Huh?" Rada said.

"Sorry, dear. I'm tired. We made loud noises with pots to scare away snakes."

Rada shivered. "I don't like snakes. Do you think we have any in our garden?"

"Perhaps."

"What else did you do?"

Baba opened her eyes and rubbed her temples. "We burned yard debris, and children jumped over the flames to protect themselves from snake bites."

"How would that protect them?" Rada asked.

Baba heaved a big sigh and closed her eyes again. "Dear, I'm weary. I'll tell you another time."

Rada rubbed her grandmother's back. "If you're tired, we can go home now. I have lots of pictures and stories to tell Mommy."

"Thank you, dear. I think that's a good idea."

Early the next morning, Rada jumped out of bed and ran to the kitchen where her parents were having breakfast. "Mommy, Daddy, I have an idea how to make Baba smile again!"

Rada's mother asked, "Sweetheart, did something happen at the zoo? Grandma ... Baba Neda looks like she's aged ten years, and she didn't say anything last night. Was she still upset about what happened yesterday?"

"No, her tree at the zoo was gone. She was sad about Diado," Rada said. "I have an idea ... if Daddy won't get mad about it."

"Why would I get mad?" her father asked.

Rada lowered her eyes. "You did yesterday. I want to start a new tradition, but I need your help."

Her father pulled her onto his lap. "I'm sorry about that. I was wrong. It's time to bring back our traditions. What do you have in mind?"

Rada whispered in his ear.

Her father's eyes twinkled. "Yes, it's perfect. I think your grandmother would like that. I'll head out and run my errand now."

"And I'll start mine." Rada jumped down and ran to her bedroom. She piled craft supplies on top of her ladybug quilt. Murka leaped onto the middle of the papers.

Rada pushed the cat aside. "Bad kitty, you'll mess up Baba's surprise."

The cat lifted her head, looked down her nose, then curled up to take a nap at the end of the bed.

The truck door slammed soon after Rada finished her project. She looked out the window, and broke into a wide grin, then raced down the stairs, waving her project to show her parents.

"That's lovely, sweetheart," her mother said. "Baba will be pleased."

"Can I get her now?" Rada bounced on her heels.

"Not yet," her father said. "Eat breakfast first, and I should be done with the task you assigned me."

Rada jiggled in her seat while she ate and kept peering out the window at her father. Finally, he nodded to her, and she ran to her grandmother's room.

"Baba, come see. We have a surprise for you." Rada grasped Baba's hand and pulled her toward the door.

"Hold on, dear. I'm in my pajamas and slippers. Let me at least put on shoes."

Baba sat on the bed, slipped off her fuzzy slippers, and slid on walking shoes.

Rada led her to the backyard, where her father leaned against a shovel by a hole in the ground. Dirt streaks covered his face.

Baba rubbed her chin. "You want to show me a hole?"

"Wait, there's more." Rada danced around her father. "Daddy, please go get it."

Rada's father went to the pickup and removed a black container.

"It's an apple tree, Baba!" Rada grabbed her hand. "We can put our martenitsi on it. Then it'll be a magic tree and have lots of fruit. It already has green leaves and white blossoms. Maybe it'll have fruit soon."

Rada's father removed the tree from the container and placed it into the hole. Rada kneeled with her parents and tossed dirt around the tree.

"I'm sure the tree's thirsty." Rada tilted a bucket and poured water around the roots, then wiped her face with a muddy hand. After she removed her red and white bracelet and tied it to a branch, she closed her eyes tight and made a silent wish.

"It's your turn, Baba. Oh, wait! I have another surprise." Rada ran into the house, leaving muddy tracks on the wooden floor.

She returned carrying objects behind her back. One by one, she tied her creations to the branches. Three black-and-white paper storks with orange beaks twirled in the breeze.

"Since we don't have real storks here, these will bring spring to us," Rada said, looking at her grandmother.

Baba smiled and cried at the same time. She bent to kiss Rada's cheek. "Thank you, sweet angel. This means the world to me. Losing the tree at the zoo felt like everything was gone: Diado, our traditions. Nothing mattered. But you've made me see it differently. Sometimes you have to let go, so something new and better can come along."

She removed her martenitsa with trembling hands and tied it to a branch. Rada's mother tied her amulet to the tree, but her father didn't wear one.

Rada wrapped her arms around his waist. "Next year, you can put one on, too. I won't let anyone pick on you for doing it. Maybe Murka will even scratch them if they try."

"Thank you, sweetheart," her father said. "This will be the beginning of our new tradition. We won't let this one die."

Baba smiled at Rada. "I'm sure Diado is watching and is proud of you, dear."

The wind picked up, and the martenitsi glided like butterflies.

Rada looked up. "Look! A stork, but they don't live here."

Baba smiled. "Miracles are created by those who believe."

Making Penda and Pijo Martenitsi

What you need:
White wool yarn or silk
Red wool yarn or silk
Small piece of cardboard, 3x3 inches
Pair of scissors
Glue gun (optional)
Plastic doll eyes (optional)

A *martenitsa* symbolizes good wishes to those you give them to. In order to make a *martenitsa*, you need white and red yarn and a lot of imagination. Let's get started and remember to have fun!

Martenitsi are decorated in various ways in different parts of Bulgaria. In southern Bulgaria, instead of white yarn, people weave in a blue thread (to guard against the evil eye). In the Rhodope Mountains, people use a few more colors.

Martenitsi are given to others to wear on March 1 as a token of friendship. Make sure you don't wear the one you made. It could make Baba Marta angry.

Step 1: Create Twisted Braid

- ➢ Cut off about 12 – 24 inches from both the red and white yarn.
- ➢ Tie the two together in a knot.
- ➢ Secure one end of the yarn with a safety pin to something that won't move.
- ➢ Hold the other end of each strand of yarn and twist them until they're tight.
- ➢ With one hand still holding the yarn at the ends you twisted, grasp the place where you tied them together.
- ➢ Release the ends that you twisted to let the two strands wrap around each other.
- ➢ Smooth out as necessary so the two strands are uniformly entwined.

Step 2: Make Pompoms

> Wind red yarn around the cardboard 10 – 15 times.

> Insert the twisted braid under all the strands at one end.

> Pull the braid together tight to compress the strands, and then tie the braid together with another piece of red yarn.

> Cut the red threads at the bottom of the opposite end of the cardboard, and remove the cardboard.

> Repeat the above process with white thread, using the other end of the twisted braid.

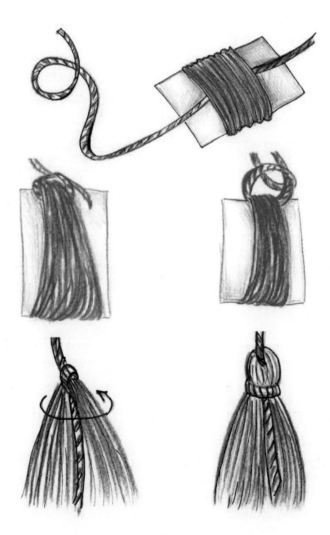

Step 3: Make Penda

- ➢ **Doll's Head**: Tie a red thread on the red pompom about 1/2 inch below the place where it's attached to the braid. The strand of yarn should be long enough so that each end reaches to the bottom of the pompom to blend in with the others.
- ➢ **Arms**: Pull out a few strands on each side of the pompom to use for the hands.
- ➢ Twist a piece of red yarn around the strands for one of the arms about 1 1/2 inches out from the body.
- ➢ Tie it tight and cut the excess yarn. Weave it in if you can.
- ➢ Repeat for the other arm.
- ➢ **Waist**: Wrap a strand of white yarn a few times around the remaining pompom about 1 1/2 inches from the top where it's attached to the thread, pulling it tight.
- ➢ Tie the yarn into a bow, or weave the ends into the "belt."
- ➢ Cut off any excess yarn.

Step 4: Make Pijo

➢ Repeat the steps from #3 (Make Penda) for the head, waist, and arms, using the opposite colors: white to tie head and arms, but red for the waist.

➢ **Legs**: Cut the bottom of the pompom so the strands are equal.

➢ Separate the threads into two equal parts.

➢ Twist a piece of white yarn around one leg about 1/4 inch from the bottom.

➢ Tie it tight and cut the excess yarn. Weave it in if you can.

➢ Repeat for the other leg.

Step 5: Add Eyes

➢ You can add eyes if you want or leave the *martenitsi* as they are.

➢ Attach two eyes to each doll with a glue gun.

www.mysticalemona.com

www.mysticalemona.com

www.mysticalemona.com

www.mysticalemona.com

www.mysticalemona.com

www.mysticalemona.com

www.mysticalemona.com

www.mysticalemona.com

www.mysticalemona.com

www.mysticalemona.com

Ronesa Aveela

Born From the Ashes

Illustrated by Nelinda

A "Baba Treasure Chest" story

www.mysticalemona.com

A steady, light tapping like a woodpecker drilling for bugs tugged at her senses.

"Kerana." Dimna's disembodied voice drifted toward her.

"No, Baba." She snuggled under the covers, closer to a black cat. "I was floating on the breeze. It was such a beautiful dream."

"Get out of bed and dressed." Her grandmother rattled the doorknob. "We have to leave before the sun rises."

She groaned and set her bare feet on the clay floor. Shivers rippled through her body. Kerana grabbed her cell phone from the nightstand. A reminder she'd left for herself flashed onto the screen: *Happy Twelfth Birthday. Maybe someone will like me this year.*

She hoped her mother would at least call since she couldn't be here.

Why couldn't she have let Kerana stay at home instead of dumping her here for the summer—in this tiny village away from everything? No, she was too busy with her big promotion to bother taking care of her daughter, and nobody else wanted to put up with a brooding child. Baba was the last resort, even though Kerana's mother didn't like her own mother.

After deleting the message, she shuffled to the door and flung it open, shoving the device close to her grandmother's face. "It's almost three a.m. Why do I have to get up in the middle of the night?"

Dimna skirted around her and stepped into the room, placing a folded white garment on the bureau. "Wear this dress."

She curled her upper lip. "I'd rather wear jeans and a T-shirt."

"It's tradition. Part of your initiation."

Kerana's heart fluttered. "Initiation into what? Mom says ..."

She studied her grandmother's outfit: a loose-fitting black dress flowed to her ankles, and a white headscarf covered her yellow, thinning hair. For a moment, she imagined flames licking a bubbling cauldron.

"You're not really a ... witch, are you?"

"Don't speak such nonsense. Your mother knows perfectly well that I'm a znahar, a healer. Get dressed so we can begin. We have a lot to do today." Dimna closed the door behind her when she left.

Kerana waited until her grandmother's slow, heavy steps faded down the hallway. She snatched the dress and hurled it onto the mattress. The black cat crawled from beneath the covers and sniffed the garment, pushing the fabric with her paw.

"Mira, stop that! Baba will be angry if you rip it." She nudged the cat away only to receive a look that said, *"You didn't treat it any better."*

She picked up the dress, rubbing her fingers on the silky softness, and brought it close to her nose. "Mmm, lavender."

After slipping it on, she examined herself in the mirror, admiring the colorful flowers and butterflies embroidered around the edge of the sleeves and V-neckline.

"Look at me." She sighed as she placed her hands against her flat chest. "A child's body in a woman's dress."

Mira's yellow eyes blinked. The cat yawned before jumping off the bed. Her tail flicking, she crouched and slunk toward the curtains, where she pounced on a spider spinning its web along the windowsill.

"You don't care either!" Kerana wiped away a tear. "I wish I had a friend to talk with, even a cat would be better than nothing."

"Kerana, hurry!" Dimna yelled.

She smoothed the crinkles from the dress as she stomped down the hallway.

Kerana tossed back her curly blond hair and thrust her hands on her hips. "I'm here. Now what?"

Dimna stopped kneading bread and sucked in her breath. "You look as wild and beautiful as a Samodiva." After wiping her floured hands on a cloth, she rose from the chair by the fireplace and hugged her granddaughter.

Kerana shrugged her off. "I'm freezing. Let me warm up a little." She rubbed her hands above the embers.

"It's summer. If you ate more, you wouldn't be so cold. What are you going to do here during the winter?"

She shrieked, "Mom's going to take me out of here before then!"

www.mysticalemona.com

Her grandmother turned away to arrange items on the hearth. "She's already kept you from me for too long. We have to do this before you reach puberty."

"Do what?" Kerana steeled her eyes on her grandmother.

Dimna pointed toward the hearth. "Kneel on the broom. It's time to perform the ritual."

"I'm not doing anything until you tell me what you're going to do."

With sparkling eyes, Dimna said, "You're going to be my successor, the next znahar."

She backed away, her eyes wide. "I won't be called a freaking witch. People at home already avoid me because they think I'm strange. They'll hate me even more if—"

"Shush, child." Her grandmother came closer and placed her hand on Kerana's shoulder, rubbing it with slow, gentle circles. "You'll have power to heal and more."

"Power? That's crazy." Kerana didn't want power. She wanted to be loved.

"It's not. You're special. The Samodivi told me."

"You mentioned them before. Who are they?"

"Kneel now. We have to hurry." Dimna again pointed to the hearth. "I'll tell you that story later."

"I don't—" Kerana stopped.

The glare on her grandmother's face scared her. She kneeled on the broom, its bristles digging into her knees.

Dimna placed a lid on the podnitza where bread dough was rising. Using an iron poker, she cleared a crevice in the middle of the ashes and placed the clay dish within it. She scooped ashes over the covered bread with an iron shovel. Her scowl relaxed when she glanced at Kerana's pale face.

"Child, don't fret. I'm not going to hurt you. I'll explain everything I do so you'll understand."

"O-okay," Kerana said without taking her eyes off her grandmother.

www.mysticalemona.com

Dimna placed the shovel on one side of the hearth and the poker on the other. "Iron tools have the power to chase away evil, especially after fire has sterilized them. Even the broom you're kneeling on is for purification because it sweeps away all unclean things."

"Why—" She shifted her knees on the broom. "Why are you doing this to me and not to Mom?"

"I failed with her when she was a child because it wasn't their wish. I won't fail with you, too."

"Their? The Samodivi?"

"Yes, now let me continue."

From a wicker basket to Kerana's right, Dimna removed three stalks of dry wheat. She plucked three grains from one stalk and placed them on Kerana's right knee, then picked three grains from another stalk, placing them on the girl's left knee. From the final stalk, she removed another three grains and tossed them into the fire.

"Wheat has been offered as a sacrifice to the gods since ancient times," Dimna said. "This will purify you so you become a vessel divine power can flow through."

Warmth crept through Kerana's body. She stared transfixed at the embers glowing in the fireplace.

Her grandmother moved behind her and grasped Kerana's shoulders. "Now repeat the incantation after me."

"Yes, Baba," Kerana replied.

With clear, slow words, Dimna spoke and Kerana echoed her response.

"From the first nymph Thrace, to me, to you,
Health from me, from God, and from the Holy Mother,
I vow to remain pure and holy, upholding the creed of the znahar,
Never intentionally harming, never for personal gain.
I will heal body, mind, and soul ..."

After a few lines, the words became a blur. Although she repeated them twice more, Kerana's mouth recited the chant, but her mind drifted away to the time of their ancestors, the Thracians. With each repetition, the world around her dissolved a little more until she was afloat above the embers, radiating their heat.

Dimna spoke from behind her. "Now make the sign of the cross three times."

"Like we do in church?"

"Yes, child, but this ritual precedes Christianity. To our ancestors, it symbolized fullness in life and a bountiful harvest. Now cross yourself."

When Kerana did, Dimna removed a clay flower from the basket and handed it to her. "Touch this to your forehead, then your heart, and finally your knees, then make the sign of the cross again."

Kerana did as instructed and extended the flower toward Dimna.

"No. Place it on your left side," Dimna said. She removed basil from the basket and stirred it in a bowl of water, all the while reciting a blessing:

"God provides everything for cures.
From me to you,
From you to others.
My hands will become your hands;
My mouth will become your mouth;
My heart will become your heart.
Forever together to bring a cure.
Your lifted hand will cure;
Your spoken word will cure;
Your gentle touch on stone will cure;
Your gentle touch on fire will cure;
Your gentle touch on water will cure.
Everything you do will bring life and health;
It will bring wellbeing to all mankind.
God and His mother will help you,
All that you do will cure.

From me to you,
From you to others.
My hands will become your hands;
My mouth will become your mouth;
My heart will become your heart.
Forever together to bring a cure.
Your lifted hand will cure;
All that you do will cure."

She sprinkled the basil water on Kerana and placed the bowl at Kerana's lips. "Drink. This will give you divine power."

After Kerana took a sip, Dimna turned the bowl a third of the way around. "Drink again."

Once more her grandmother moved the bowl, and Kerana drank. "This will guide your mouth to speak, your hands to do, and your heart to feel everything that brings health and life to others."

"How?" Kerana whispered.

"Understanding will come in time."

Dimna brushed ashes off the clay dish and removed it from the fire. As she lifted the cover, a tantalizing aroma from the golden-crusted bread wafted around Kerana.

"This is dobra dusha, kind soul," Dimna said as she broke off three pieces. "The first is the mediator that transfers power from me to you."

Her grandmother ate the piece, then handed a second one to Kerana. "Eat this."

The warm bread dissolved in her mouth, and her mind exploded with thoughts and visions. She felt alive and free.

Dimna placed the final piece of bread high in the chimney. When done, she sat in the chair next to Kerana. "We now share the power of healing. You will receive all my power when I die, and you will continue the family tradition. You may now rise, my heiress."

She got up and stood in front of her grandmother. Dimna tied a red thread around Kerana's right wrist and pinned a geranium onto her dress. "These will protect you when we go out to collect herbs."

K erana set her willow basket on the ground so she could yank a thorny vine from her sleeve. A full moon shone on the bushes and other undergrowth crowding the forest path. "Baba, where are we going? It feels like we've been walking for hours."

"Hush, child. The forest is full of eyes and ears. We're almost to my secret herb garden."

Scooting closer, Kerana whispered, "Why couldn't we wait until it was light out?"

"Today is Eniovden, Midsummer's Day. Herbs collected close to dawn have magical power."

Kerana twisted the red thread. "How will this and the flower protect me?"

"Red is the sun's strength. They'll protect you from the evil eye." Dimna stopped and looked among the trees. "And the Samodivi."

Kerana shuddered. "Are you going to tell me who they are now?"

"They're nymphs who protect the woods, fields, and waters." Dimna crossed herself as she continued walking. "I met them where my garden is now. They taught me everything I know about healing. My grandmother had dedicated me to them when I was an infant. When it was time for my own initiation, she brought me here. The Samodivi made me their sister and gave me the gift of healing."

"Then why do I need protection from them?"

"They don't accept all humans. Depending on their mood, they would just as soon capture you to join them as they would want to make you go insane with their seductive voices." Dimna stepped into a clearing. "Here we are. Let's hurry and collect herbs. We need seventy-seven and a half different kinds."

"Why that number? A half herb is rather strange."

"Each herb has a remedy to cure one of the seventy-seven known illnesses that exist. The half herb is for any unknown ailment." Dimna bent and broke off herbs, placing them in her basket. "We'll use some to make a giant wreath along with the other women in the village. Every Eniovden, young girls step through it in a special ceremony."

Kerana remained silent while they collected the herbs, wondering how bad a fit her mother would have when she discovered what her grandmother had done.

"Please fill this with water." Dimna handed Kerana a copper kettle engraved with the sun, moon, and stars. "Then put the herbs in it and leave it by the porch steps."

She lugged the heavy kettle outside and set it down.

"Move it away from the house a little more," Dimna instructed. "It needs to sit under the stars for the rest of the night so the herbs are even more powerful."

"I thought being a znahar would be more exciting than this," Kerana mumbled as she pulled the kettle toward an open space. "Here okay?"

"Yes, that's fine. Now come inside. I have something important to give you."

She leaned against the door after she closed it. "Why didn't you teach Mom all this?"

"Your mother wanted nothing to do with our traditions. Even at a young age, she had grand plans. She was going to leave this little village and change the world." Dimna wiped away a tear. "And she broke my heart doing it."

"And you think I'm different? I grew up in the city where people believe in modern medicine, not ... magical herbs."

"Yes, you are different. Not everyone can understand the healing power of herbs. A person has to have a gift before she can be a znahar. I tried to force it on my daughter, even though the Samodivi told me to wait a generation before passing on the knowledge."

www.mysticalemona.com

"Mom never told me why she kept me away from you. What was she afraid of? This inheritance? Or do you have other secrets you're not telling me?"

"Wait here. My gift will give you a clearer understanding."

Dimna removed a key from the pocket of her dress and unlocked a large, metal padlock from a door off the kitchen.

"Why do you keep that door locked?" she asked.

Dimna turned her head toward Kerana. "I have powerful herbs in here. They'd be dangerous to anyone not knowing how to use them."

"How ...?" Kerana began, but her grandmother had already closed the door behind her.

She pressed her ear against the door. Inside, papers rustled and glass clinked. Her grandmother's heavy steps got louder, so Kerana scurried to sit in a chair. Dimna carried a tattered book with a leather cover.

"Baba, you're so secretive. What is that?"

Dimna set the book in front of Kerana. Her fingers trembled as she placed her granddaughter's hands on the cover. A tingling sensation vibrated through Kerana.

"My dear child, I'm getting old. This is the book of knowledge. It lists the herbs and their incantations." Dimna sat next to Kerana. "You must promise me not to tell anyone the spells. They'll lose their power if you do."

Kerana caressed the book, longing to open it. "I promise. Are you sure you're not a witch? Mom says it's evil."

"Don't pay attention to her. Ignorant people use the word 'evil' for things they don't understand." Dimna sighed. "My purpose in life is to heal as many village people as I can, not only their physical problems, but also emotional and spiritual ones. When they want to bear children, they come to me. When they want prosperous crops, they come to me. When the waters dry up, they come to me. I keep bad spirits away from the village. Some people are afraid of me because of these things, but they respect me, knowing I'm here to help them."

"Thank you, Baba." She wrapped her arms around her grandmother. "You make me feel special."

"You are, my dear. You were born to be a znahar, to help people." Dimna stood. "I'm tired. I'm going to rest before the Eniovden festivities at the school. I'll begin teaching you afterwards. You should get some sleep, too. The sun will be up soon, and we still have a busy day ahead of us."

"I will, Baba. Is it okay for me to look through the book a little first?"

"Yes, but don't read it out loud until you can feel the herbs in your soul. Each one will speak to you what healing cure God gave it." Dimna stopped at her bedroom door. "If you touch the herbs and speak the words before you have this knowledge, their magic can harm or even kill you or the person you're trying to cure."

Kerana thumbed through the book's frayed, yellowed pages, with Mira curled next to her on the bed. Mindful of her grandmother's warning not to say the words out loud, she silently read penciled notes scribbled next to drawings of plants.

Herbs, like humans, have vitality. Merely plucking an herb does not release its energy. God endowed each plant with the ability to communicate. The color of its flowers, the shape of its roots and leaves, and the type of stem are used to determine its healing capacity. Yellow flowers heal jaundice. Plants with red leaves or roots are essential for blood-related diseases. The leaves of a purple iris can reduce the effects of bruises. Flowers shaped like butterflies can lessen the sting of insect bites. But the flower alone cannot cure without the proper words recited at the time of healing.

Kerana read remedies and spells for making love potions and preventing a person from falling asleep. She raised her eyebrows when she read the specifics of Angelical: *This herb is associated with the angels. Therefore, it's used to protect people from evil spells or demonic attacks.*

"Vervain!" She laughed when she read the next one. "I've heard of this from vampire shows. This says it enhances magical powers and prevents attacks against the mind. I guess that fits. It prevented the vamps from controlling humans. What do you think of that, Mira?" She stroked the cat's back.

Mira stretched, yawned, and purred.

"I'm getting tired, too." She yawned, but her eyes continued to ravage the pages, each one more fascinating than the last.

She flipped to the next page. "With Nostrum, you can break down a stone wall. I don't know why I'd want to do that. What else?" Kerana yawned again. "One more. Elecampane liquid lets you communicate with animals."

Kerana sat up, startling Mira. The cat hissed and jumped off the bed.

Once again, she read the passage. "It would be so cool to talk with animals. I wonder if Baba has any of this."

She slipped out of bed and tip-toed toward the herb room. The metal lock wasn't closed. Grinning, she opened the door slowly, but the hinges squeaked.

"Why aren't you sleeping, child?" Dimna said with a groggy voice from her bedroom.

"I'm thirsty and wanted a glass of water."

Kerana paused, listening until her grandmother's breathing became steady. She stepped inside the forbidden room.

Dawn was breaking, lighting the room. Fragrant, dry herbs hung in bouquets along the back wall. A glint on the table caught her attention, and she checked it out. A golden cross was submerged in a flat copper bowl filled with water. Not what she wanted. What else was in the room?

A bookcase held multi-colored glass jars. "What's in this?" She peered at a shriveled snake head and shivered. "Gross. And that one looks like a bat. Where are the herbs?"

She squatted and read labels from the jars on the lower shelf. Geum, White Oman, Nostrum, Elecampane.

www.mysticalemona.com

Kerana's heart pounded. "That's it!"

With a trembling hand, she opened the purple bottle and sniffed. No smell.

She took a small sip and smacked her lips at its slight sweetness. "Maybe a little more."

"Kerana, finish your drink and go to bed," her grandmother's muffled voice said. "You'll be overtired for the celebration later."

Startled, Kerana almost dropped the jar. "Don't get up! I'm going now. Good night."

She quickly screwed on the cover and replaced the bottle on the shelf. After closing the door, she hurried to her room and picked up the cat from her bed.

"Mira, talk to me."

The cat opened her eyes and yawned.

Kerana frowned. "I'm so stupid to believe in this magic stuff. It's nonsense. Herbs can't let you talk with animals."

She crawled into bed and buried herself under the cold blankets.

K erana woke to a rough tongue licking her face and sharp pinpricks on her shoulder. Whiskers tickled her nose, and she sneezed. She opened her eyes to find Mira staring at her through yellow glass slits.

"Get up, dormouse. I'm hungry."

Kerana jumped out of bed. "Who spoke? Nobody's in the room."

"Well, I'm here." Mira swished her tail.

"I must be dreaming, or ... the herb worked!" Kerana snatched the cat from the bed. "Mira, say something else. Please tell me something."

"Let me go, Kerana. I'm hungry, and you've overslept."

"Yes, the herb worked!" She jumped around the room, then stopped. "I can't tell Baba. She'd be angry I used the herbs before she taught me."

She went into the kitchen, fed Mira, and kissed her grandmother.

"Happy birthday, dear," Dimna said. "With all the excitement this morning, I forgot to wish you health and blessings, and may all your wishes come true."

"Thanks. Today one did come true." Kerana smiled.

She had a friend to talk with.

After breakfast, Dimna and Kerana removed half the herbs from the kettle and wove them into a long strand.

"I'll dry the rest for my medicines." Dimna patted her wet hands on a towel. "Take this one to the school."

Kerana dropped the herbs. "You're not going with me? I don't know anyone there."

www.mysticalemona.com

"I'll be there later, but I have things to do here first."

"We can go together."

"No, the women need these herbs for their wreath." Dimna placed it into Kerana's hands. "There are plenty of girls your age you can talk with. They'll all be going through the ceremony."

Her shoulders slumped. "Another ceremony? Are they ... becoming znahars? I thought you said it was special, that I was special."

Dimna hugged her. "You are. This is a different ceremony to ensure our young women are protected from the zmey."

Kerana opened her mouth to ask what a zmey was, but her grandmother continued, "He's a dragon who likes to kidnap young girls when they're dancing. Not to be mean, of course. He has a tender heart and often falls in love with human maidens, and wants to marry them."

Kerana laughed. "Surely that can't be true."

Dimna curled her lips into a knowing smile. "Tell you what. Let me give you a quick znahar lesson. Grab a bowl and spoon, and join me outside."

It had lightly rained during the time Kerana had slept. Puddles formed pools around the driveway.

Dimna kneeled near one, and she motioned Kerana over. "The morning of Eniovden, I always gather dew or rainwater. It acquires healing power after the sun bathes in it. I use this water to make potions."

"Can we make something after the ceremony?" Kerana scooped water into the bowl.

"Yes, perhaps a cure for insecurity," Dimna said, her eyes filled with sadness.

Wearing the white, embroidered dress, Kerana yelled from the door, "I'm leaving. If Mom calls, tell her I miss her and love her."

She grabbed the twisted herbs and dragged her feet toward the school. Laughing and shouting filled the playground.

www.mysticalemona.com

She squeezed the herbs close to her chest and took a deep breath. "I can do this."

A dark-haired girl, wearing a dress similar to Kerana's, ran toward her. "Hi, I'm Sophia."

"I'm Kerana. My grandmother's—"

"The znahar. Everyone knows her." Sophia took Kerana's hand. "Come with me. We've been waiting for her herbs. They have special protection powers."

"Do you really believe a dragon will steal you to make you his bride?" she asked.

Sophia shivered. "I don't want to find out. Did you know the zmey's bride eventually grows a tail like his? One girl tried to bite hers off when she wanted to visit her family. She thought they'd be afraid, or even ashamed of her for running off and marrying a dragon."

"Were they?"

Sophia sighed. "She never made it home. When she heard her former friends singing down the road, the poor girl was in a frenzy to remove the tail before they saw her. She tore away at it so fast that her heart burst, and she died. It never ends well falling in love with a dragon."

"At least she had friends once," Kerana mumbled.

"You'll make lots of friends here." Sophia squeezed her hand. "I can already tell you're going to be my best friend."

The large room where women and girls twisted herbs onto a wreath smelled heavenly.

Kerana opened her eyes wide. "Wow, that's huge!"

Sophia laughed. "It has to be so we can walk through it."

"How do you add the herbs to it?"

"Like this." Sophia showed her.

Kerana picked up a bunch of twisted herbs and looked for a place to join in. The women and girls busily chatted away as they went about their task. Kerana hesitated and set the herbs down. "Sophia, I'm going outside to wait for Baba. Come sit with me when you're done."

"Don't you want to help?"

Kerana shrugged. "I don't want to miss Baba when she gets here."

Sophia hugged her. "Okay, I'll be there shortly. I'm not letting you get out of stepping through the wreath. I'd hate for a zmey to steal you from me."

Kerana sat at a picnic bench under a gnarled oak. Children swarmed like bees around the playground, some waving to her. A flock of birds on top of the old school roof distracted her as they squawked and flew off in a rush. A couple of ravens landed on a branch above her and ruffled their feathers.

"I told you it was dangerous to land on the roof. Why don't you ever listen to me? Someone's been pecking at that wire and now it's exposed. Didn't you notice the sparks? It almost burned my feet."

"Yah, well my wing got burned, too. The flames licked my beautiful feathers."

Kerana jerked her head toward the birds. "What flames? What do you mean?"

The two birds looked down. The larger one said, "Who are you?"

"I know. I know." The other bird hopped on the branch. "She's the gifted one, Dimna's granddaughter."

"What about the flames?" Kerana asked. "Where are they?"

"On the school roof. Sparks from an exposed wire have ignited the roof," the smaller bird said.

In exasperation, Kerana yelled, "You said that already, but what part of the roof?"

"Hey, who are you talking to?" A boy riding a bicycle circled the tree. "Oh, you're the witch's granddaughter. Is she hiding in the tree with her broomstick?"

"Leave me alone." She glared at the heavyset boy, and took a deep breath, inching her way around him. "Real witches don't fly on brooms. They pickle heads of mean boys."

"Yah, and then you eat them. Either that or you fly around the forest to collect bats for dinner," the boy jeered. "You're a witch like your grandmother. I saw you both flying on brooms last night."

"Get lost, stupid boy. I have to go," Kerana said as she rushed off. "There's a fire in the school."

"What? Who told you that? I didn't see a fire."

"The ra— I just know there's one." The boy would think she was crazy, or maybe even decide she was a witch if knew she could talk with animals.

"Fire! Fire!" Kerana screamed as she neared the school. "Get everyone out!"

Several people rushed outside, but a woman standing by the door grabbed Kerana's shoulder, pulling her aside. "What are you talking about? There's no fire."

"The roof's on fire! Please believe me. I-I saw smoke up there. You have to get everyone outside now."

"She's crazy like her old witch grandmother, Mrs. Dimova." The boy laughed as he swaggered over. "She was jabbering away to nobody a moment ago."

Kerana started crying. "Please tell everyone they have to leave the building."

The fire alarm sounded, wiping the smug grin from the boy's face.

A thunderous crack came from over the cafeteria, and the roof collapsed. Glass shattered as the walls crumpled. Flames lurched from the gaps, hissing like a seven-headed dragon.

Mrs. Dimova pulled Kerana and the boy outside well away from the building, then dialed the fire department. "Everyone stay calm. The firefighters are on their way. Check to see if anyone you were with is missing."

Kerana looked for Sophia amid the frantic people shouting and screaming in the schoolyard.

A white mouse brushed against Kerana's trembling leg. "So much smoke. Your friend screaming. Door locked. Trapped."

She kneeled by the shaking creature. "Sophia? Where?"

"In the biology lab."

She sprinted toward the building.

A man grabbed her arm as she ran past. "Where are you going? The building's going to collapse at any moment."

"Let me go or she'll die." She kicked him in the shin, and he yelped, releasing his grasp.

People were still swarming out of the building. Children screamed for their parents. People pushed against each other as everyone scrambled past her toward the exit like frightened sheep.

"Where's the lab?" Kerana asked one person.

He pointed down a long hallway.

The intense heat bit at Kerana's skin. She groaned, inching a beam away from the door. A sea of smoke poured out, stinging her eyes. She coughed. "I'm here, Sophia. Where are you?"

Crying came from the wall next to her. She reached over and felt a body. Sophia's ash-smudged face peered at her.

"Thank God, you're safe." Kerana grabbed her hands. "Hurry now. Let's get out of here."

They were almost at the door when a beam cracked above them. Kerana pushed Sophia forward. "Go!"

A flame burst between them, blocking Kerana from the door. Sophia froze.

"Go! Now! I'll find another way out."

Another beam cracked and flames licked the air. Sophia screamed, "I'll get help," and raced out the door.

Smoke choked Kerana, and she collapsed.

"I love you, Mom. I love you, Baba."

Scorching heat and blinding light surrounded Kerana before darkness overtook her.

Firefighters raked through ashes and burning embers, all that remained of the school, looking for a body. One picked up a burned cell phone by the place where the front door of the school used to be. He handed it to the chief.

"I'm so sorry for your loss, ma'am. We couldn't find Kerana's body. She was brave and saved another girl, but lost her own."

"Oh Lord, my child." Dimna trembled, tears running down her face.

Mrs. Dimova wrapped her arm around Dimna. "No one believed her about the fire. How could she have known?"

"My Kerana was special. Where are you, my sweet child?"

"I'm here, Baba, trapped under a beam. Please help me." She struggled to make her way to the surface. Ash toppled to the side as she poked her head out. "Fresh air at last."

She waved to the people standing a few feet in front of her. Her grandmother continued to weep.

"Can't you see me, Baba? I'm right here."

Kerana beat against the ashes that encased her like a cocoon. "I'm so weak. Got. To. Try. Harder."

She wiggled around more until she was delivered from her ashen tomb. "I'm free."

"Look. What's that moving in the ash?" Mrs. Dimova asked.

A beautiful butterfly with red-and-black-striped wings like a burning flame rose from the ash. It perched on Dimna's arm for a moment, then spread its wings and fluttered on the breeze.

"I love you, Baba. Tell Mom I love her, too." She was free to soar higher than she'd ever thought.

***

In honor of Kerana and her heroism, villagers planted a colorful herb garden in front of the new school. Every summer a red-and-black butterfly with flaming wings returns to the place where her freedom began.

www.mysticalemona.com

www.mysticalemona.com

www.mysticalemona.com

www.mysticalemona.com

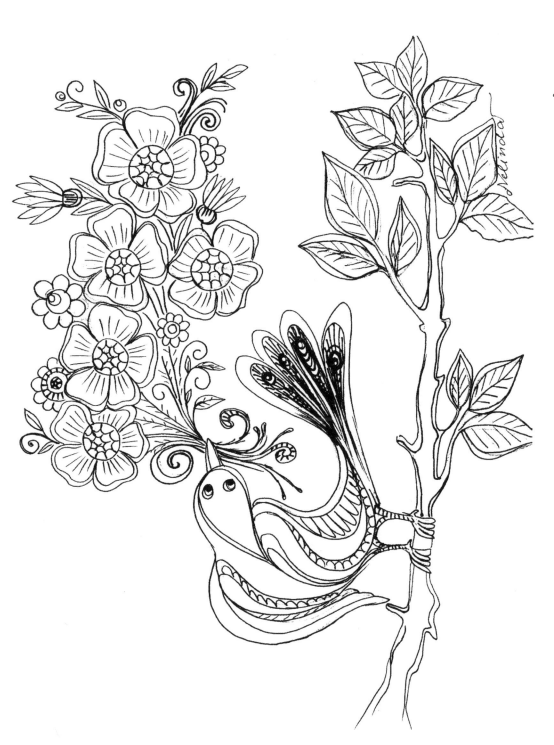

www.mysticalemona.com

www.mysticalemona.com

www.mysticalemona.com

www.mysticalemona.com

www.mysticalemona.com

www.mysticalemona.com

Nelinda

Ronesa Aveela

Mermaid's Gift

Illustrated by Nelinda

A "Baba Treasure Chest" story

I cicles on the school's eaves dripped onto Nick as he hurried toward the basketball court, clutching a ball to his chest. His best friend George ran close behind. They dumped their backpacks at the base of a pine and wiggled out of their jackets. Laughter and giggling filled the schoolyard as other children played tag, climbed the jungle gym, or swung while waiting for parents to pick them up.

"I'm first," Nick shouted and dribbled the ball onto the court.

He dodged George, who made a swipe to steal the ball. Nick jumped and tossed the ball toward the hoop. It hit the backboard, missed the basket, and flew onto the court. Both boys scrambled after the ball yelling, "Mine!"

Lunging first, George landed with a thud on the ball. Nick toppled onto him.

George groaned. "Umph! Get off."

Nick rolled off, laughing, and helped George up. "Guess it's yours after all. Last hoop. My mom should be here soon."

"Why do you have to leave so early?" George puffed out a frosty breath. "If we want to play like Michael Jordan, we have to practice more."

"Mom invited guests for my Name Day, and I have to help her get ready."

"Name Day? What's that?"

"It's like a birthday," Nick said.

George dribbled the ball. "You just had your ninth birthday in October. It's only been two months, so it can't be a half birthday."

Nick shook his head. "Nah, a Name Day's more popular for Bulgarians. It's a really old tradition."

"Your family's always celebrating something."

A car horn tooted, and Nick glanced toward the road. "It's Mom. Gotta go. Why don't you come tonight, and I'll tell you more?"

George frowned. "I don't have a gift."

"You don't need one for a Name Day. When my grandmother was young, people just stopped by. Now, since we're busy, we invite guests."

The car horn beeped longer.

Nick grabbed his jacket and backpack. "Mom's in a hurry. Promise you'll come?"

George nodded and looked at the sky. "Okay, if my parents let me. Mom says a storm's coming tonight."

At the third horn blast, Nick ran to the car and slid into the backseat. He rolled down the window and shouted, "Come anyway. You can stay over."

His mother sighed as he rolled up the window. "We're already going to have a houseful."

"All the kids are older than me." Nick pursed his lips. "Except the twins, and they're three."

"You should try to get along with your cousins."

Nick snorted and buckled his seatbelt. "They're annoying girls, and they break my toys. I wish Uncle Peter would leave them home."

"You know he can't do that," his mother said as she put on the turn signal, looked to make sure no traffic was coming, and pulled onto the road.

Nick leaned forward and rested his hands on his mother's headrest. "You know, if I got a puppy as a present, they couldn't break it."

His mother looked in the rearview mirror, a scowl on her face. "We've had this conversation too many times. With all the hours your father and I work, we don't have time to take care of a pet."

"But, Mom, I will—"

"Don't argue. I have enough on my mind worrying about your father out at sea."

Nick let out a long breath. "He's not home yet?"

"No, he and his crew are still fishing for cod off the Misery Islands." Her voice quivered as she looked at the dark clouds gathering over the ocean. "All the stations say we're in for a gale storm tonight. Your grandfather's rickety boat is so old and slow. I don't know why your father insists on keeping it."

"Dad's been in storms before. He'll be okay."

"St. Nicholas willing." His mother crossed herself.

"Huh?" Nick said. "How's he going to help Dad?"

"Since he's the patron-saint of sailors and fishermen, if we pay homage to the saint today, he'll protect us."

"Will I be a saint, too, since I celebrate the same Name Day?"

His mother shook her head. "Don't be silly." She parked in front of an Italian bakery and took money from her purse. "Please run inside and get the bread I ordered. It's the last thing on my list."

Nick frowned. "You're not going to make the bread this year? I love your *pitka*."

She shook her head. "I'll barely have time to prepare the carp."

"But the bread's special," Nick said. "Do Italians know how to make Bulgarian ritual bread?"

"Yes, don't worry. I gave him our recipe and pictures of how to decorate it."

"Isn't that cheating? I thought you had to make the bread yourself?"

"According to tradition, we do, but sometimes people create their own traditions," his mother said. "We keep them alive to understand who we are. Anyone who doesn't know his heritage is like a boat without an anchor, floating in the ocean and searching for a pier."

She handed Nick the money. "Now, please get the bread so we can hurry home."

Nick uncovered the bread when he got back into the car. The baker had decorated the top with images of fish. He sniffed it. "Mmm, smells great, and it's as pretty as yours."

T he car crawled along the highway. Sleet pelting the vehicles slowed the Friday rush-hour traffic even more. The windshield wipers squeaked as they kept a steady rhythm. By the time they reached home, the precipitation had turned to drizzle, and a dense fog covered the neighborhood.

Nick carried in the bread, while his mother gathered shopping bags.

"Dad," Nick shouted after he rushed inside. No one replied, and he bit his lower lip. "He's still not home."

"Check the answering machine, please, while I get the rest of the groceries."

Nick listened and shook his head when his mother returned. "The only message was from the town saying the Christmas tree lighting is next Sunday."

His mother shivered. "Will you put the salads into bowls while I call the Coast Guard to look for your Dad?"

Nick stared at her with big eyes. "You think he's lost?"

"I'm sure he's fine," she said while craning her neck to look out the window toward the ocean, "but I want to give them a heads up that he's out there just in case."

Nick scooped the different kinds of salads into colorful bowls, then unwrapped the carp. It stared at him with bulging eyes and an open mouth, with a look that said, "Let me go."

His mother stopped at the front door after making her call. "Oh, Nick, you've tracked muddy water all over the house." She threw open a closet door, and it banged against the wall. Knick-knacks on a shelf rattled. "I have only two hours to get everything ready. I don't have time to clean up your messes."

"I'll do it." Nick took the mop from his mother's trembling hands. "Is the Coast Guard going to look for Dad?"

She shook her head and dropped into a chair, giving him a faint smile. With a sad, soft voice, she said, "The storm's too bad at sea to go out right now. They said not to worry since they haven't received any distress signals."

"Should we cancel the party?" Nick asked.

His mother took a deep breath. "No, everyone's already on the way from Connecticut."

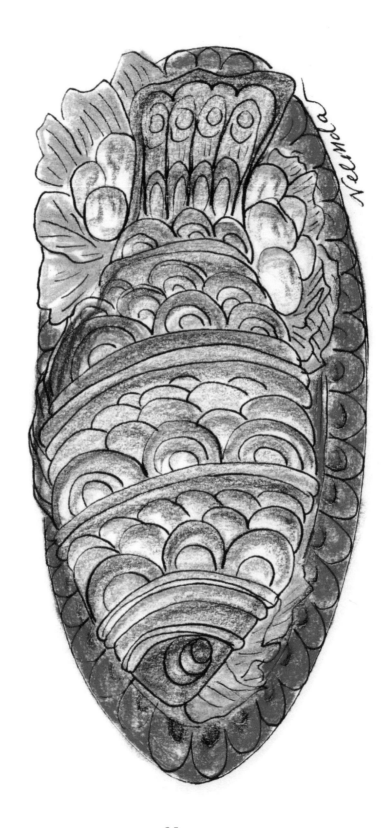

"But I want Dad here."

His mother heaved herself from the chair and smoothed out her clothes. "I'm sure your father will be home soon. St. Nicholas will keep him safe."

Nick furrowed his brow. "Maybe he made the weather bad because you didn't make the bread." He looked up at his mother and quickly added, "But I'm sure he'll be happy after you make the *ribnik*."

"Yes, that should make him merciful and protect our fishermen."

She shuffled to the counter, where she prepared dough to wrap around the carp. On the top, she added a series of half circles, decorating the fish to look like scales. When she finished, she put it into the oven.

Next, she lit candles, handing one to Nick. "Help me by putting these on the shelves and tables."

Nick sniffed the air. "Mmm. Smells like cookies."

"They're vanilla. It'll get rid of the damp odor." She opened the door under the sink and removed a white plastic bag. "Speaking of smells, please throw the garbage out, then come right back."

The rain had slowed, but a gusty wind licked Nick's cheeks when he opened the door. He trudged down the steps and tossed the bag into the trash bin, closing the lid tight so raccoons wouldn't get inside. Looking toward the ocean, he wondered if his father's boat was at the slip yet. The neighbor's wooden fence blocked his view, so he climbed on a bench and peered over it.

Dense fog obscured the ocean. While he clung to the fence, lightning shattered the sky and thunder boomed directly overhead. Startled, Nick jumped off the bench. Icy raindrops pattered against the trashcan. The sleet-covered grass crunched as he ran back into the warm house.

A festive white tablecloth, embroidered along the edges with fish, seahorses, and shells, covered the table.

His mother wiped her hands on a dish towel, her expression taut as she looked out the window at the streaks of lightning. Her voice cracked when she said, "Nick, please set the table."

He arranged the plates, napkins, and forks, then helped with chopping vegetables and fruit, while his mother prepared appetizers. The oven dinged, and Nick's mother removed the *ribnik*.

Nick licked his lips. "That smells great."

His mouth watered as he looked at the table. The carp took center stage, with the bread, salads, appetizers, and a bottle of wine surrounding it.

Nick's mother let out a long breath. "Finished. One more thing I need to do before our guests arrive. I have a special gift for you, Nick. I'll get it while you change into something festive."

"What is it? Sneakers like Michael Jordan's ... or a puppy?"

She narrowed her eyes and shook her head. "Don't start that again. No puppy, but maybe your father will get you those sneakers." She peered out the window and sighed, her eyes filled with worry. "I'm sure he'll be here any minute."

A few moments later, Nick's mother knocked at his bedroom door as he slid on a clean, white shirt.

"Come in," he said.

His mother sat on the bed and patted for him to sit next to her. Her fingers stroked a patinated brass box, decorated with mermaids surrounding a ship in a storm.

"I've waited until I felt you were grown up enough to understand the value of this gift."

Nick stared at the box. "What is it?"

The cover creaked as his mother opened it and withdrew a compass.

"This belonged to Grandpa Nikola. Now it's yours. He always said it was magical and helped him find his way home."

"Awesome!" Nick opened the lid.

Aquamarine crystals glittered around the outside of the compass. Inside, black navigational points stood out against a blue background. He twisted the compass, trying to be quick enough to make the arrow point in a different direction.

Nick looked up. "Where'd Grandpa get it?"

"He wouldn't say. Rescuers found him clutching it when they pulled him out of the water after his ship went down," she said. "The people who saved him said the only word he spoke was 'Assyria.' He never told us what he meant."

"Thanks, Mom." Nick clutched the compass. He had dreamed of being a captain of a ship like his grandfather and traveling around the world. "This is the best gift ever."

She smiled and ruffled his hair. "Better than a puppy?"

"Well ... I still want a puppy."

"Take good care of the compass, and it'll protect you, too."

"I'll guard it with my life." Nick hugged his mother.

The doorbell interrupted them, and his mother went to welcome their guests. Nick fiddled with a key dangling at the end of a golden chain, imagining that it opened a treasure chest. He turned the compass to the back side. Writing formed a circle around a smiling mermaid sitting on a rock. Aquamarine crystals, like those on the front, sparkled in her eyes. He brought the compass closer to a desk lamp and peered at the tiny words: *Nothing is more precious than life.*

His mother called up the stairs. "Nick, George is here."

He shoved the compass in his pocket and rushed down the stairs. "Hey, George. Can you stay over?"

George shook his head. "My mom will be back in an hour."

"Only an hour?" Nick groaned. "That means I'll have to entertain the twins when you leave."

"Mom didn't want to drive at all, saying the weather was going to get even worse. I had to keep pestering her until she gave in."

"Let me show you what I got." Nick reached into his pocket as the doorbell rang again.

His mother poked her head out of the kitchen. "Nick, will you get that?"

"Sure," he called to her, then turned back to George. "I'll show you later."

A gusty wind blew papers off a hallway table when Nick opened the door. His grandmother huddled under the covered entryway, her arms wrapped around her waist. Behind her, Nick's Uncle Peter and Aunt Sophia each held one of the twin girls, who were already whining.

His grandmother squeezed past him out of the cold while his aunt and uncle set the twins down inside. The girls squealed and scrambled straight up the stairs toward Nick's room.

"Oh no." He groaned, glad he had taken the compass with him so the twins wouldn't destroy it.

His grandmother hugged him. "Happy Name Day, Nick. Let your name live forever. Be healthy and happy. Here's a little gift for you."

"Thank you, Baba." He took the wrapped gift.

His grandmother shivered. "I'm going to sit by the fire and warm my old bones until we're ready to eat."

While Nick's aunt helped Baba take off her coat, a crash came from upstairs. Nick cringed. With an apologetic smile, his aunt hurried after the twins.

His uncle scowled as he removed his coat and hung it on a hook. "We'll replace whatever they broke this time."

Nick shrugged. "I hope it wasn't one of my favorite ships in a bottle."

"Maybe this will take your mind off whatever they broke." His Uncle Peter handed him a huge, wrapped package. "Happy Name Day. Let your name live forever. Be healthy and happy."

George joined Nick. "So what's this Name Day stuff? I thought it wasn't a birthday or half-birthday, and you didn't get gifts."

"Nice to see you again, George." Uncle Peter grinned. "A Name Day is more important than a birthday, and, no, you don't have to bring gifts. We don't see Nick that often, so we like to bring him something on his special day."

"Why's it more important?" George asked.

Uncle Peter scratched his chin. "I guess because it's also a celebration of a saint's feast day. Today is St. Nicholas Day, so it's the Name Day for anyone with a similar name, like Nick here."

"Hey, St. Nick. You're like Santa." George tapped Nick on the shoulder. "Do you have a St. George? I want a party, too."

Uncle Peter nodded. "Indeed, there is. St. George is famous for killing a dragon. His feast day is May 6."

George smiled. "I can have an outside party with dragons." He paused, looked up at Uncle Peter, and spoke softly, "Can I celebrate a Name Day even if I'm not Bulgarian?"

"Of course, you can," Uncle Peter said.

"Awesome!" George punched his fist in the air. "But I'm going to tell people they're supposed to bring presents."

Uncle Peter laughed. "You two go play. I want to talk with your father, Nick. Where is he?"

"He's not home from fishing yet," Nick said as he put the gifts from his grandmother and uncle on a table.

Nick's mother came into the hallway. "I've called the Coast Guard a couple of times. They still don't have any news."

"Oh dear." Baba rose from the couch and crossed herself. "Every time your grandfather was at sea, I prayed for St. Nicholas to protect him."

"And he always came home safely," Uncle Peter said, "even that one time his ship sank."

Baba nodded her head vigorously. "If St. Nicholas had been on the ship with them, I'm sure the saint would have prayed, and a carp would have jumped out of the water to fill the hole, the way one did in legends."

George covered his mouth to stop his laughter. "A fish stopped a ship from sinking?"

Nick nudged him to be quiet, then whispered, "Yes, carp are considered servants of St. Nicholas. They'll do whatever he asks."

Putting her arm around Baba's waist, Nick's mother said, "Let's not stay in the hallway. The food's ready."

Aunt Sophia came down the stairs, carrying a squirming twin under each arm. She looked at Nick. "They broke a vase in the hallway."

He sighed with relief.

His aunt set the twins on chairs in the kitchen where the others had gathered. "What a festive table! The bread and fish are gorgeous. I have to take a picture." She removed her cell phone from her purse.

Nick's mother covered her forehead. "Please tell me you're not going to post this on Instagram."

"No, it's just a memory for the girls when they get older."

Aunt Sophia took a picture. "Now one with everyone." She looked around. "Where's David?"

"Fishing," Nick said.

"In this storm?" Aunt Sophia said. "Is he crazy?"

The room went quiet, intensifying the howling wind and rain pelting the windows.

Uncle Peter leaned close to Nick's mother. "Do you want me to go to the wharf and look for him?"

She shook her head. "I'm sure he'll be fine. If he had made it back, he'd be here already. Let's eat before the food gets cold."

The adults loaded their plates, chatting quietly as they walked around the house. Even the twins behaved while eating in silence at a small side table. They seemed to feel the anxiety of the others.

More family and friends continued to arrive, filling the house with laughter. Nick received a lot of kisses on his cheeks and many "Let your name live forever" wishes. Colorful packages began to pile up on the hallway table.

Little by little, the beverages, carp, and ritual bread dwindled. All that was left of the fish was the bones.

"Better grab a bone while you can," one of Nick's cousins said.

A rush of children ran toward the fish, plucking off bones to put into their pockets. The adults also picked at the carp and deposited bones in bags and purses.

George looked sideways at Nick. "Why do they want bones?"

"Carp bones are sacred and are supposed to bring good luck."

"Huh? Fish bones can be sacred?"

"Carp ones, anyway." Nick pointed to a bone in the fish's head. "See, it's shaped like a cross. On my first Name Day, my mom sewed the cross bone into my baby hat to protect me."

George shook his head. "You have some strange customs, but I'm still going to ask my mom if I can have a Name Day celebration in May."

Nick's mother poked her head into the kitchen. "Speaking of your mother, she's here and waiting in the car."

"Thanks," George said, then turned back to Nick. "See you tomorrow if the storm stops."

"Okay. Maybe we can go sledding."

George rolled his eyes. "You're dreaming. The rain washed away all the snow."

"If it turns colder tonight, it might snow."

"Doubt it," George added. "My mom said we won't even have snow for Christmas. She's a weather bug and is usually right."

"Maybe it'll snow as a gift for me?" Nick said.

George looked wistfully at the stacks of colorfully wrapped presents on the table. "Looks like you already got a bunch of stuff. Hope there's something good and no clothes."

Nick sighed. "The best gift I could get is for Dad to come home safe."

"With St. Nicholas on your side, he'll be okay," George said. "And, geeze, I think your mom called the Coast Guard a hundred times."

"She's worried, and so am I."

"I know, but when the fog lifts, they'll search for the boat and send helicopters out. It's not like a hundred years ago. He's probably riding out the storm farther out at sea."

A car horn tooted. George waved his index finger. "In a minute." He turned back to Nick. "What were you going to show me earlier?"

"A cool compass my mom gave me." Nick pulled it from his pocket and opened it. "And a key to a treasure chest."

"Awesome." George examined the objects. "We'll have to see if we can find it."

George's mother beeped the car horn three times.

"Gotta go. See you tomorrow." George ran down the steps, opened the car door, and jumped in.

Nick went back into the house. The noise was unbearable. The twins were screeching, and all the other kids were shouting. No one acted concerned about his father except him, his mom, Baba, and Uncle Peter. His mother talked with the guests, but kept looking out the windows. Baba followed her around, crossing herself, and saying St. Nicholas would protect him. Uncle Peter pulled Nick's mother into a hug from time to time.

Nothing is more precious than life rolled around Nick's head. He couldn't stand the noise any longer, so he grabbed his jacket and scarf and slipped out into the cold, windy night. The streets were empty. Only the lights from George's mom's car flashed at the end of the street. The American and Irish flags on their neighbor's house flapped against the metal poles in the wind.

"Dad, where are you?"

If no one else was going to look for his father, Nick decided he would. The pier wasn't far. If he ran on the trails between the houses, he could get there in less than ten minutes. His mother wouldn't notice his absence if he hurried back. Nick peeked in a window, then stole away down the steps toward the pier to see if his father had returned.

The wind bit into Nick's cheeks by the time he neared the water. A seagull sitting on a post squawked, alerting a colony of gulls huddled at the end of the pier. They flew over the roiling ocean, scolding him for disturbing their rest.

Nick panted as he bent over, putting his hands on his knees while he caught his breath. Waves churned high, battering the boats moored like a row of gulls. His father's slip was empty. Streaks of lightning flashed in the dense fog far out at sea.

"Dad, where are you?"

The crashing waves and wind swallowed his voice.

Nick removed the compass from his pocket. "Mom said you're magical. Show me how to save my dad and get him home." He read the words from the back aloud: "Nothing is more precious than life."

The brass arrow jumped between North and South like a fish trying to find its way home.

Nick banged it against his palm, then checked again. The arrow still twirled around. "Aw, man, it's broken."

Shivering from the cold, Nick decided to return home so his mother wouldn't worry. He pocketed the compass and took a few steps down the pier.

Something splashed in the water behind him. He turned around, hoping his father's boat had returned.

The slip remained empty.

Another splash came from the side of the pier. It was too cold and stormy for a person to be swimming. Maybe a seal had been washed close to shore.

As Nick stared into the darkness, a woman's head appeared out of the water. A crown of shells, pearls, and tiny starfish adorned her hair. She grasped the wooden platform with her milky-white hands. Green and blue fins cascaded from her wrist to her elbow. It must be a costume, Nick thought.

"Are you okay?" He went closer and looked over the edge of the pier.

She swished her long, red hair to the side, removed seaweed from her shoulders, and smiled at him, showing pearly teeth.

The woman's head disappeared beneath the water, and another splash sounded behind him. He twirled around as a green and blue fish tail dipped below the surface. Icy drops of water splashed his face. He rubbed them away and glanced where the tail had sunk beneath the water. The woman rose and smiled at him again.

"Who are you?" he spluttered while his heart raced. "Why are you in the water?"

"I'm a *rusalka*, a mermaid. The ocean's my home."

Nick rubbed his eyes. He must be dreaming. When he looked again, the woman still clung to the edge of the pier. "Mermaid? They're only in fairy tales."

She shook her head, still smiling. "Mermaids have existed for thousands of years."

"I think you bought one of those fake tails from the internet."

The woman flipped her tail. "Touch it if you want. It's real."

Nick kneeled on the pier and reached out his hand. He hesitated over the scales. They looked real, but couldn't be, could they? He lowered his fingertips and skimmed their surface. Gasping, he quickly drew his hand away, clutching it to his chest as if burned.

"That's not a costume. They're rough and slimy," he said.

"Hmph." The mermaid sneered. "Now do you believe me?"

"Um, maybe." Nick bit his lower lip. "Who are you?"

"My name is Assyria. I'm—"

"Who?" Nick opened his eyes wide. "My grandfather repeated that word when he was rescued."

Assyria laughed, the sound like a symphony of tiny bells. "He was talking about me."

"How's that possible?" Nick looked at her closer. "You're too young. That happened forty years ago."

"I'm a hundred, the youngest of seven sisters."

Nick hit the side of his head. Water must have clogged his ears. "Why did you help my grandfather? I thought mermaids drowned humans."

She sighed, twirling a tendril of hair. "My sisters wanted to drown him, but I loved him. He was such a handsome man—and strong. I watched him every time he went out to sea. I disappointed my sisters by finding him a raft to float on."

"Why are you here now? Did you come back for him? He's ... in heaven."

"No, I came because you called me."

"I didn't!" Nick gulped a lump in his throat. "How could I have? I didn't know you existed."

"You called me with the compass. I came to fulfill a vow, Nick."

He leaped back, almost falling into the water on the opposite side. "How do you know who I am?"

"I always know the name of the person carrying the compass," Assyria said. "Don't be afraid. I'm here to help you. What is it you desire?"

Catching his breath, Nick stared at her. Could she really help? "Can you tell me where my father's fishing boat is?" he asked, his voice trembling. "He hasn't come home, and my family's worried."

Assyria dove into the ocean, sending a spray of water onto the already soaked pier.

"Don't leave!" Nick peered into the dark, swirling eddies. "You said you'd help."

For a long time, he stared at the spot where she had disappeared. Resigned that she wasn't coming back, he shuffled down the pier with his shoulders hunched.

"Nick," Assyria called him back. "I've returned."

He whipped around. The mermaid sat on the edge of the pier, splashing her tail in the water. She held a large sea snail's shell in her hand.

"I can call my sisters with Trident's trumpet." She pointed to the shell. "They'll search the seas for the boat and guide it to shore. But you must give me something valuable in return."

"I don't have money with me, but I can go home and get some from my mother."

"You humans think you can buy everything with money." Assyria's eyes saddened. "It has no value in my world. I desire something that's precious to you: the compass."

Nick stuck his hand in his pocket and fumbled with his mother's gift. "I can't give you that. Anything but the compass. It belonged to my grandfather. You can have my basketball trophy, or a signed poster of Michael Jordan, or my ship in a bottle."

"It must be the compass." Assyria held out her hand. "It was a gift from me to your grandfather and was meant to be used only once. Now you must return it."

"How do I know you gave it to him?" Nick clutched the compass.

Assyria didn't withdraw her hand. "Give it to me, and I'll show you."

The wind picked up, blowing ice particles against Nick's face, and waves swelled around him. The ocean seemed angry. Had Assyria done that?

He ran his thumb over the compass cover. "I promised my mother I'd guard it with my life. She'll be upset if I give it to you. I have to keep my promise."

"Is it more important than your father's life?" Assyria asked before she slid off the pier and slipped beneath the water.

Nick ran to where she had sat, and dropped to his knees, splashing his hand in the water. "Come back! You can have it."

Green, blue, and red streaks rippled through the waves as Assyria swam back. Her green eyes sparkling, she pulled herself onto the pier next to Nick.

"The compass, please." She stretched her hand toward him.

With a racing heart, Nick pulled the compass from his pocket and held it toward her in his palm.

The touch of her long, sharp fingernails against his skin made him shiver.

Assyria turned the compass around, and flicked one of the aquamarine crystals from the mermaid's eye. A shiny tear formed below her own eye.

"These crystals are tears I shed for your grandfather. I offered him eternity, but he wouldn't stay with me." She heaved a sigh. "He said another had captured his heart, and his love waited for him at home. My tears in the compass protected him."

"Those are your tears?" Nick looked at her in wonder.

"Yes, now that I have the compass again, I am free to shed more." She wiped away the tear, and it dropped to the pier, forming a crystal again.

"Now to uphold my promise." Assyria lifted the conch to her lips and blew. It made a noise like a hissing cat. She held it to her ears, listening. "My sisters know where your father's boat is."

"Is he okay?" Nick held his breath.

"Yes. The storm disabled their navigation equipment, and because of the fog, they couldn't find their way to shore. My sisters will guide the men home."

She picked up the dropped tear and placed it onto Nick's palm. "Remember me."

Giving Nick one last smile, she dove into the icy, black water. Her fish tail flashed above the waves as if in farewell, then disappeared.

Nick blinked twice. What just happened? Was it real? He patted his pocket where he had put the compass. It was gone. He squeezed his hand tight and felt an object there. The mermaid tear Assyria had given him.

What was he going to tell his mother? He stared out toward the ocean, waiting for his father's safe return.

"Nick," his mother shouted as she ran down the pier, her coat unbuttoned. His Uncle Peter trailed her.

Nick rose and wrapped arms around her trembling body.

"I was scared out of my wits," she said. "We looked all over the house for you. It's bad enough I'm worried about your father. I didn't need to wonder what happened to you. What are you doing here?"

"Sorry." Nick hung his head. "I wanted to see if Dad had come back."

"You can't do anything out here in the storm. The Coast Guard would have let us know if they had news." She shook her head. "And look at you. You didn't even put on boots. You'll catch pneumonia for sure. Let's get you home."

Nick pulled away. "Please let me stay. Dad will be home soon. Assyria promised she'd help."

"Assyria?" Nick's mother looked at him with confusion.

"The person Grandpa talked about after he was rescued." Nick bounced on his feet. "She's a mermaid."

"Oh, Lord, you are sick. Do you have a fever?" His mother touched his forehead. "We have to go home quick."

"No, Mom, it's the truth. Look, she gave me this." He opened his hand and showed her the crystal.

His mother picked it up and scowled. "Is that from your grandfather's compass? Did you break it? I shouldn't have given it to you yet."

"It's a mermaid tear, from Assyria. Honest." Nick grabbed it back. "I had to give her the compass so she'd save Dad."

"We'll talk about this later." She turned to Uncle Peter. "Please take Nick home. I need a few moments to calm down."

A horn blasted from out in the ocean. They all turned to look. Two rows of silver flashes flicked on and off like runway guide lights. In the middle of them, a white bow emerged from the fog like the *Flying Dutchman*. The words on the side read *Elenore*.

"It's Dad! I knew it. Assyria promised to help him." Nick took a step toward the boat, but his mother grabbed hold of his hand.

The boat eased into the slip. Once it was docked, the men tied ropes and let down the anchor. Nick's father jumped onto the pier, his crew following as they unloaded their catch.

A crew member waved Nick's father away when he started to help. "Captain, go to your family. We'll clean up and put the fish on ice."

"David!" Nick's mother rushed into his arms, with Nick right behind her. "I was so worried."

He hugged them both tight, smelling of salt, fresh fish, and seaweed. "What a day. Do I have a story to tell you."

Splash after splash came from beyond the pier. Silver tails flicked in and out of the water like a school of minnows. Nick's father saluted them until they disappeared.

"You're not going to believe me when I tell you," Nick's father said.

Nick grinned. "Mermaids."

His father opened his eyes wide, then nodded. "Mermaids."

Nick's mother huffed. "I know it's his Name Day, but don't encourage the boy with his fantasy."

David shrugged and said, "Happy Name Day, Nick. I didn't get a chance to get you the ocean map I promised. We'll go shopping tomorrow. You can have that or whatever you want."

"Except a puppy," his mother chimed in.

David nodded. "Except a puppy."

"You're home, Dad. That's the best gift of all." For what was more precious than the life of someone you loved?

Nick felt someone staring at his back. He turned around. The silhouette of a red-haired mermaid at the end of the pier waved before disappearing into the water.

He was sad he lost his grandfather's magical compass, but happy his father had returned safe.

"Dad, let's go home. Mom made a ton of food for my Name Day, and lots of people came. I saved you some *ribnik* and a bone for good luck."

Something icy pinched Nick's cheeks. He looked up at the sky. Tiny white flakes floated down.

"Snow! George and I can go sledding tomorrow." Nick danced in front of his parents and took his father's hand as if he never wanted to let him go.

"This is a night full of wonders," Nick's father said.

Ronesa Aveela

THE Christmas Thief

Illustrated by Nelinda

A "Baba Treasure Chest" story

 wet nose tickled Christopher's cheek. He wrapped his arms around the beagle and whispered, "Did you know today's a special day? It's Christmas! I get presents and can eat cookies and Grandma Nona's fortune bread."

He jumped out of bed, ran to the frosty window, and breathed on it until the warmth melted a peephole. The ground was a blanket of white, and decorated homes covered with fluffy snow looked like sugar-coated gingerbread houses.

"Skipper, it's snowing!"

"Woof, woof." The dog nudged his pajama bottoms and thumped his tail against the floor, looking up with pleading brown eyes.

"Wanna go outside? I want to make snowmen and have snowball fights."

Christopher turned away from the window, but frowned when he caught a glimpse of himself in the dresser mirror. "I look like a girl in these pajamas, but Mom says I have to wear them because Grandma Nona bought them."

The dog sniffed the pink bunny slippers, turned up his nose, and nodded in agreement.

The smell of freshly baked cookies and apple pie floated into his room. Christopher shouted, "Race you!" He dashed toward the stairs, with Skipper nipping at his heels.

"Wait!" Christopher stopped and grabbed hold of Skipper's collar. He gazed at the railing decorated with pine branches. "I wanted to slide down so I could win."

With a quick look at Skipper, he said, "Ready, go!" He released the dog and bunny-hopped from one step to the next. The floppy slipper ears tripped him, and he slid down the rest of the way. Christopher lay in a heap on the floor with Skipper licking his face.

Christopher sat up, and wiped off doggie drool with his sleeve. "I know. You won."

He dashed into the living room and skidded to a stop. The Christmas tree glittered with golden bows and glass ornaments, and a star on top twinkled. Christopher lowered his gaze to the gifts wrapped in shiny paper. He poked a few with mysterious shapes, then his breath caught and his heart throbbed.

The blue bicycle he had dreamed about leaned against the wall.

He raced toward it and traced his fingers over the shiny wheels and rims, lingering a moment on the seat. "Rrrmmm, rrrmmm." He twisted the handlebars.

"Mooooom!" He burst into the kitchen. "Mom, Mom, Santa brought me the bike I wanted!"

"Good morning, my love. Merry Christmas." She turned from the hot stove to face him. "What an infectious smile! Just like your father's. You even have his sparkling blue eyes and dimples."

Her face, hair, and apron powdered with flour and her fingers covered with dough didn't prevent Christopher from wrapping his arms around her and cuddling close. Skipper scampered around, wagging his tail so fast they could hardly see it. He almost knocked Christopher and his mother off-balance.

She laughed. "I'm sure you got a lot of nice presents because Santa knows you've been a good boy this year."

"Can I open them now?" He squeezed his mother tighter.

"Not until after supper, when your father returns with Grandma Nona."

"Ohhh." Christopher released his mother and eyed the towering plate of chocolate-chip pancakes on the counter. He stuck his nose close to them. "Mmmm. Can I have one?" He dipped his finger into a bowl filled with warm chocolate.

"It might be Christmas, but you know the rules. First brush your teeth, wash, and get dressed."

Christopher hurried to his room, quickly got dressed and cleaned up, then rushed back to the kitchen. He gobbled his pancakes.

"Can I go outside and play with Ania, now?" he said after swallowing the last bite. "I want to show her my new bike."

"Help me get food ready first."

He shook his head, ran to the living room, and clung to the bike. "I want to go outside."

"Christopher ..." His mother followed. "I know you're excited, but I have so much to do still—roasting turkeys, baking pies ... and Grandma Nona's special fortune bread."

She sat in a chair next to him and tilted his face so he looked into her warm, hazel eyes.

"Sorry, Mom. I'll help." With a lingering look at his bike, he sighed, then returned to the kitchen.

After finishing his chores, Christopher scrambled into his jacket, pulled on warm gloves, and dragged his bicycle to the door.

"Christopher, you can't take the bike out right now." His mother put her hand on his shoulder. "It's too icy. When the roads are clearer, you can, but not now."

"But—"

His mother held a finger up. "You can ride it in the house later on, but go tell Ania about it now."

He shuffled as he returned the bike, then went outside. Skipper trotted behind, his leash making a trail through the snow. Christopher's breath puffed out in misty clouds as he ran down the street, and his cheeks tingled in the chilly air. He waved to Ania, who was making a snowman with her younger brother, Robbie.

She waved back. "Do you like our snowman? Look at his pointy carrot nose, and Mom gave me two lumps of coal for his eyes." She removed her tattered red scarf and wrapped it around the snowman's neck. "There, that's better."

"It's awesome!"

"Wanna help me with his buttons?" She cupped her hands, breathing on her red fingers and held them to her rosy cheeks.

"Don't you have gloves?"

She put her hands inside the pockets of her worn brown coat. "I'm okay. I love to play in the snow without gloves."

"Ania, guess what?" Christopher broke into a wide grin. "Santa brought me a bike! I've wanted one for so long."

Her mouth quivered and her eyes filled with tears. "I don't think Santa got our letters. Robbie and I were good all year, but we didn't get any gifts."

Robbie hit the snowman. "He musta put us on his naughty list."

"Um." Christopher shrugged and looked away. *Ania couldn't have been bad. Robbie maybe, but not Ania.*

She wiped a tear with the back of her hand. "But Dad's not so sick. That's a better Christmas gift than toys." She grabbed Robbie's hand when her mother called to her. "Well, we gotta go. Bye." She dragged her brother into their house.

Christopher picked up Skipper's leash and walked farther down the street toward another group of children who were pelting each other with snowballs from behind snowbanks. He ducked as one flew past him. He toppled behind the snowbank and joined the fun, while Skipper chased after the snowy missiles.

All too quickly his mother called to him from the doorway. "Christopher, come inside now for lunch."

Christopher breathed in deeply after he entered the kitchen, where his mother sang while she dashed around. "It smells delicious."

A turkey roasted in the oven, while another cooled on the counter, along with two pies. Trays of cookies sat on the counter ready for baking.

"Can I have a piece of pie?"

"For dessert. Right now you can have hot chicken soup after you wash your hands."

"Do you think the Winter Monster will steal the extra turkey, pie, and cookies?"

The previous year they had disappeared from the porch while they were cooling off.

"I'm seven now. I can keep the Monster away and make sure he doesn't take anything."

"I'm proud of you. You're so brave." His mother smiled at him.

All afternoon Christopher cruised from the living room to the kitchen on his bike. "Mom, watch me!" he shouted each time he passed her.

Car doors slammed in the driveway.

His mother looked out the window. "Christopher, go get the door for your father and Grandma Nona."

He hopped off the bike and leaned it against the wall.

Christopher ran to the door and threw it open. "Grandma, Santa brought me a bike! I want to show you." He grabbed her hand and dragged her toward the living room.

"Slow down." She laughed. "Let me take my coat off first."

"Let me help you." He unfastened the lower buttons.

Grandma Nona hung the coat on a hook, then bent to hug and kiss Christopher. "Look at you. You've grown. Let me see that bike now."

"Watch me ride it." He scooted on the seat and pumped at the pedals.

"You're quite the big boy." Grandma Nona breathed deep. "Your lovely tree smells like a *borova gora*."

Christopher stopped the bike. "Huh?" His grandma sometimes used words from her native language.

His father stepped into the room. "It's Bulgarian for 'pine forest.' "

"Dad, see the bike Santa brought?" Christopher circled his father.

"I see." His father grasped the bike handles. "It's time to put it in the hallway so you don't run over anyone."

Christopher frowned, but obeyed. "I helped with the turkeys and cookies. I'm gonna make sure the Winter Monster doesn't get them."

His parents shared a smile.

"Christopher, please carry Grandma Nona's suitcase to her room, then wash for dinner," his mother said.

As he headed up the stairs, his mother carried a box with a turkey, pic, and cookies to the porch.

Christopher rushed upstairs with Skipper on his heels. "I have to guard the food from the Winter Monster."

He opened his chest of toys and pulled out a bow, two arrows, and his Batman mask, then snuck downstairs. He wiggled into his jacket and crept onto the porch, closing the door quietly.

The box with the food was still there. His stomach rumbled and his mouth watered from the smell of turkey. He hid behind the barbecue grill and waited in the quiet night. The bright moonlight reflected off the snow. His hands began to freeze, but he still waited holding the bow.

Soon footsteps crunched softly through the drifts.

It must be the Monster!

Christopher trembled and chills swept through his body. He notched an arrow in the bow and held it tight. His heart pounded fast while he held his breath.

The frozen wooden stairs creaked. He wanted to scream, but he peeked around the barbeque grill. A silhouette appeared. It didn't look like a Monster. More like a person. But a scarf covered its head, so he couldn't tell who it was. The person picked up the box of food and limped away with heavy steps.

Christopher waited a few minutes in his hiding place, and then quietly followed the thief. The silhouette slid through a fence and went into Ania's house. When the door opened, he saw the person's face. It was Ania's mother.

Why is she stealing our food?

Christopher threw the bow on the porch and stormed into his house. Stamping his feet as he ran into the living room, he shouted, "Dad, I know who stole the turkey! I saw her! Mom, Moooom!"

Christopher's father set his newspaper on the table and looked at him with a kind smile. His mother came out of the kitchen, her brows creased.

"Mom! Dad! I saw who stole the turkey. Ania's mother. I hid and followed her. The Winter Monster isn't—"

"Christopher!" His father patted his lap. "Come sit with me."

With Christopher's head leaning against his chest, his father spoke softly. "Calm down. Ania's mother didn't steal the food. Your mother prepared it for their Christmas dinner. Their father's ill and can't work. We share our food so they can have a nice meal."

Christopher wiped away tears, then hugged his father. He looked at all the boxes of gifts under the tree. "I have so many toys. I can give some of my gifts to Ania and Robbie. Santa didn't get their letter."

His parents looked at each other and smiled.

"It's too late tonight. Tomorrow morning you can visit them. I promise. But don't bring up the food. It might embarrass them." His father rubbed Christopher's head. "Let's eat now."

Christopher's father broke pieces from Grandma Nona's special holiday bread and handed one to everyone and set two on a small plate. "Let's see what our fortunes say."

"Skipper gets a piece, doesn't he?" Christopher asked, as the dog's tail thumped against the floor.

"Not to eat, but he has a fortune, too." His mother broke apart one of the pieces of bread sitting on the plate, reading the foil-wrapped note inside, "A year free of trouble."

"Who get the other one on the plate?" Christopher asked.

"That's for the entire household," Grandma Nona answered. "Whatever it says applies to everyone."

"I love this game." Christopher dug into his piece of bread to extract the foil-lined fortune. "I got the coin! I'm going to be rich!"

He stuffed the coin in his pocket. When no one was looking, he snuck a piece of the bread to Skipper, and whispered, "I think I'll give the coin to Ania. I want to share my fortune with her."

Christopher looked from one happy face to the other. He thought about Ania's family and their bad luck, and hoped they enjoyed their meal as much as he did. His mother was the best cook in the world, after all.

His parents made him proud. This was the true meaning of Christmas: to be with your family and share your fortune with those in need.

What are some of your family rituals? What rituals did you love as a child?

_____

_____

_____

_____

_____

_____

_____

_____

_____

_____

_____

_____

www.mysticalemona.com

UNSCRAMBLE THESE WORDS

NEDSRIF

_____

REHAS KEYTUR

_____

SINGSLEBS

_____

www.mysticalemona.com

What is your favorite Family Tradition?
Do you have ideas for new traditions?
Write your ideas and share!

_____

_____

_____

_____

_____

_____

_____

_____

_____

_____

_____

_____

www.mysticalemona.com

Help Skipper find his present

UNSCRAMBLE THESE WORDS

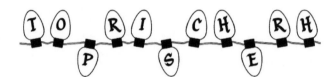

_____

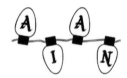

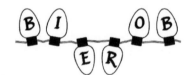

_____

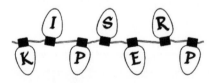

_____

www.mysticalemona.com

Your Time to SHINE

How many words can you
make from the letters in:

CHRISTMAS

_____

_____

_____

_____

_____

_____

_____

_____

_____

_____

www.mysticalemona.com

Help Christopher
Find His Bike

www.mysticalemona.com

Design a Christmas Sweater for Christopher

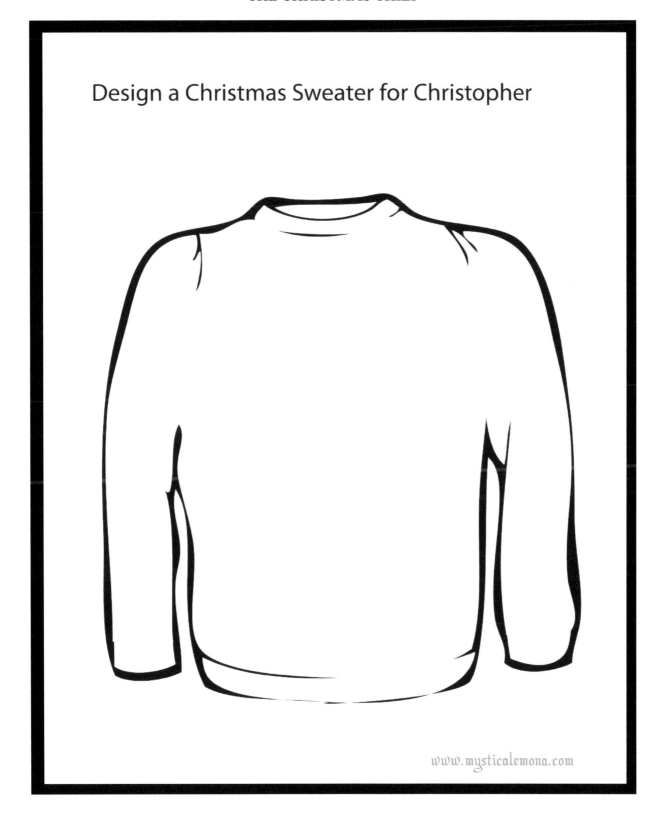

www.mysticalemona.com

Write "Merry Christmas" in different languages

Every year Christmas is celebrated in many countries all over the world. Saying "Merry Christmas" in a different language is a fun way to impress your friends!!!

www.mysticalemona.com

www.mysticalemona.com

www.mysticalemona.com

www.mysticalemona.com

www.mysticalemona.com

www.mysticalemona.com

About the Author

Ronesa Aveela is a freelance artist and writer who likes writing mystery romance inspired by legends and tales. In her free time she paints. Her artistic interests include the female figure, Greek and Thracian mythology, folklore tales, and the natural world interpreted through her eyes. Ronesa is married and has two children.

Ronesa's Books

Mystical Emona: Soul's Journey
Light Love Rituals: Bulgarian Myths, Legends, and Folklore
The Unborn Hero of Dragon Village

Baba Treasure Chest series
The Christmas Thief
The Miracle Stork
Born From the Ashes
Mermaid's Gift

Adult Coloring Books
Mermaids Around the World
More Mermaids Around the World

Cookbook
Mediterranean & Bulgarian Cuisine: 12 Easy Traditional Favorites

Reviews

Please consider leaving a review to help indie authors. Thank you.